THE RULES OF THE RACE

THE
RULES
OF THE
RACE

**THE POWER OF COMPETITIVE STRATEGY
TO SHAPE BUSINESS SUCCESS**

BRAD ARCHER, MD

LIONCREST
PUBLISHING

THE RULES OF THE RACE
The Power of Competitive Strategy to Shape Business Success

FIRST EDITION

ISBN 978-1-5445-3563-0 *Hardcover*
      978-1-5445-3564-7 *Paperback*
      978-1-5445-3565-4 *Ebook*

CONTENTS

INTRODUCTION

Year after year, I sat down in the boardroom with the rest of the executive team for our annual strategic and operational planning cycle. In this particular year, the thought occurred to me that there was something missing from our conversations. It had nagged at me for the last few years, and I had finally realized what it was.

For the prior few months, I had been reading articles from the *Harvard Business Review, Journal of Marketing Research, Association for Psychological Science, Current Medicine Sports Reports*, and more on the topic of competition. Of course, everyone in business knows that competition is important, but while I was planning out the strategic direction of my hospital, a light bulb went on. Why have we never done a competitive analysis on *ourselves*? How would a self-competitive analysis be done?

I went home, and over the next few months, I started combing through the available literature on the topic, but

I couldn't find anything that simply and clearly spelled out how to create a competitive analysis and summary of your own company. There were studies and examples, but, like a physician who wants to find a diagnosis, I wanted to put this idea into a framework that could be repeated.

In discussions with friends across various industries, I'd ask them for their thoughts on competition and how they approached it. The ones who were business owners didn't have a framework. The ones who worked in a large company didn't know how their company even approached the topic. I asked them how they contributed to or participated each year in the company's strategic and operational planning cycle. The most common answer: budget. That was their only participation.

To me, that was bizarre. You're a frontline manager over a department or division that's integral to the company, but you don't know how the company approaches competition?

Small business owners know that understanding competition is important, but it's a vague notion. There's no framework, no strategic plan. After having this discussion with a few dozen people, I realized that there was a need for a simplified framework that I could use to have this discussion with people—because it's essential to the mission of a company. It's a fascinating topic that not enough people know about or fully understand, at least not in the business world.

I realized that politicians seem to do this innately. They know the election cycle is time-limited, so they have to carefully consider how they are going to sell themselves and how they are going to handle the competition. In fact, politicians stretch the entire spectrum of potential competitive behaviors (that you'll learn about in part three). They consider: *can I win by touting myself and what I can do, or do I need to attack the other person and eliminate the competition? Am I going to devise comprehensive policies and establish solid credentials and then defend them, or am I going to go all-in on a negative campaign and aim to destroy them on several major topics?* This thought approach, which comes as second nature to politicians, needs to be applied to every business venture.

I used a combination of my clinical thought process of how to structure a clinical question and how to categorize a clinical diagnosis to come up with a "treatment plan." (This is an approach I use with most problems in my life.)

Since the first iteration of this framework, it has evolved and adapted, and now, it's ready to share with the world.

YOUR PROBLEM

To put it simply, you don't have a competitive position for your company—you may not even know what a competitive position is—and that lack of knowledge is actively damaging your success.

By not defining your competitive position, you aren't receiving maximum output from your employees. They don't have a clear direction on what actions they should or should not take or how their current actions are impacting the future of the company. You may believe that your sales team is following one strategy when, in reality, the sales incentives you've given them tell them that they should be following a completely different strategy—most likely one where the focus is on eradicating the competition. Their drive to reach these incentives is hurting your company's position in the market.

You have inconsistencies across the spectrum of activity your employees are taking, and you can't figure out why. The reason—which we'll discuss in more detail—is that every single person has a different reaction to competition. We're all competitive, but how we respond to it depends on the strength of our personal identity and social categorization, our past, and our genetic makeup. This means that your sales team is putting a competitor out of business because they see your competitive position as being the only option in the market. But your finance team hasn't budgeted to take on a segment of the market that that competitor handles, and you don't—a segment that would require your company to add new equipment and overhead—because they don't see the competition as something to be eradicated.

These inconsistencies have resulted in friction across departments and potentially a company-ending financial disaster when you are forced to enter a segment of the market that you are not ready to enter.

Your mission statement defines who you are as a company, why your organization exists, and the impact you want to have on your world. It tells customers and employees your aspirational journey of significance. But it is incomplete if it does not also clearly state your organization's competitive strategy. In fact, you could be undermining your mission (and impacting the company's financial output) without meaning to because of this gap in your knowledge.

THE MARBLE GAME

Competition can be detrimental to profits. As far back as the 1950s, studies show that a competitive orientation adopted by business managers actually resulted in less profit for the company and a higher probability of going out of business.

One study, which started in the fifties and continued into the eighties, assessed the competitive atmosphere of several companies, trying to answer the question: was each company being compared to their competition, or were they focusing more on individual profits? Each company was then classified based on their actions. Researchers watched these companies over three decades to see who had the highest profitability, who stood the test of time, and who struggled. They found that the companies with a goal of capturing sales or a goal to beat the competition in a specific area would do that to the detriment of profit. The companies focused on profit also stood the test of time and survived, where the majority of those focused on market share failed.

In another such study, researchers would tell participants one of two mission statements. The first option was, "Your job is to acquire as many marbles as possible." The second option was, "Your job is to beat your competitor."

They found that participants who were told the first option almost always ended up with more marbles than participants told the second option. Those participants were sacrificing their marbles in their attempt to win at all costs.

If your mission statement is to acquire as many marbles as possible, but your incentives are telling your sales team to win at all costs, your company is going to end up with fewer marbles than it could or should acquire because your mission statement and competitive position are not in alignment.

THE SOLUTION

Your question now becomes, what do I do if I know that I need a competitive position but don't have one or fully understand what it is? The solution is in your hands right now: this book.

I wrote this book to give business owners and entrepreneurs a straightforward way to view your company's competitive position in a way that aligns with your company's mission. You'll understand the importance of not only having a competitive position but communicating it with every employee in the company, so everyone is on the same page, increasing cultural coherence and financial output. This book provides a simple framework to start with, which you can then customize to your company's specific industry and requirements.

WHAT YOU'LL LEARN

My extensive career in the medical industry means that when I see a cluster of symptoms and the resulting physiological change, I have an overwhelming need to uncover the correct diagnosis and then create a treatment plan that is individualized to that patient. If I prescribe a treatment to a patient and they tell me that it's not working, I'm not going to insist that they keep trying it anyway. We re-evaluate the situation, what did and did not work with the last treatment, and devise a new treatment plan.

Similarly, this book is a simplified structure for what is a nuanced and complicated topic that needs to be individualized for each company that uses it.

In the first part of the book, you'll learn what a competitive position is, why it's important, what factors affect it from both biological and behavioral standpoints, and how it influences your company internally and its interactions with the market.

In the second part of the book, you'll learn how to approach a competitive position using three basic possibilities that can be used as a base and expanded upon to fit your company, industry, and market situation.

In the third part of the book, you'll learn how to create your own competitive position, basing it on your mission statement, and how to ensure the entire company understands it, creating company cohesion. Then, we'll end with ways you can react to your competitors' strategies.

WHY I WROTE THIS BOOK

A few years ago, I was just like you. I had never considered the official competitive position of the companies I was working for—in fact, I didn't know that competitive position existed. However, as I was looking back at my decades in the medical business, I realized that something was missing.

As I went through life, I would notice weird behavioral actions happen, both at the companies I worked at and at my competition, which would make me think, *Why would this person (or organization) take that action?* I followed this trail of thinking and looked for the story behind this person or that organization, searching for the missing piece that would make this action logical.

Strategic planning is a normal part of every business. And there has been copious amounts of material created on the importance of competitive intelligence. However, those two topics have never been combined. There is no simple framework for businesses to use in order to approach it.

Like many of you, I'm a business leader in my company, and I'm driven by and concerned about the technical aspects of my business. No matter what industry you are in or how large your business is, you need to focus on the technical details relative to your particular business, but the importance of thinking about your competitive position is not stressed or even described in common literature. I discovered this gap and realized I had no good way to think about this—and there was no book or course I could turn to in order to learn it.

So I decided to write it myself.

A little about my educational and business background. I specialized in pharmacy for my undergrad with the idea that it was the business I wanted to go into. At that time (enough years ago that I don't want to give a date), most pharmacies were independent, small businesses. However, while I was in pharmacy school, big names like CVS and Walgreens started taking over, and small pharmacies became virtually extinct.

I had no interest in working for a chain corporation, but I did have a general interest in the scientific aspects of medicine, so I pivoted from pharmacy school to medical school, specializing in internal medicine for adults with acute and chronic illnesses. I practiced as a private, boarded physician for over twenty years until the last several years when I started to devote more of my time to administration as the Chief Medical Officer.

Along the way, I received a Master's degree in Healthcare Delivery Service from the Dartmouth Institute. Essentially, it's a combination of their public health and business schools, which teaches you how to run a hospital.

At Dartmouth, I learned the importance of a comprehensive strategic and operational planning process. Case analyses provided an opportunity to look for subtle details in instances of success and failure. This approach, taught by world-renowned experts, sparked my curiosity about the motivational elements of human behavior in business. It's a phenomenal school, and they taught me a lot, including covering a lot of information about competition in general.

It was because they taught so much about competition that I was able to see a gap.

Over the last eight years, I started putting together presentations on competitive position for local businesses. However, I wasn't reaching enough people—I wasn't helping enough people—and the idea for this book came to life.

WHAT THIS BOOK IS AND ISN'T

I hope this book will be a trigger for you to think about your company's mission in a different, more holistic way. It should be used as a starting point, a way to see the dichotomy between your incentives and the boardroom discussions and begin to align your operations. It's a primer on the topic of competitive position in business.

It is not a hard and fast scientific study. It is not the only way to approach this idea. There are hundreds of different ways for you to tackle your competitive position. I encourage you to use this book as a base and then find your own way forward.

There's a lot of academic writing on competition. When you read it, you think, *Oh yeah, that's good.* But then, when you go to work the next day, how do you implement that knowledge? The aim of this book is to bridge the gap from vague awareness to actionable steps.

And the first step on this journey is to understand what competition really means.

PART ONE

COMPETITION BASICS

CHAPTER ONE

WHAT IS COMPETITION?

Zelensky Brothers Cleaning was a cleaning service company that started as an insurgent in a regional market. Although they initially focused on providing better service, they niched down, in the beginning, to decide who their primary customer would be—a normal process for new businesses—and because they didn't have a full scope of services, such as major disaster cleanup and chemical spills.

To handle these problems, they outsourced to a larger, more established company as a subcontractor. This allowed them to still offer all of the services they were expected to offer while reducing their overhead investment and keeping a higher profit margin.

In fact, there was no intention of ever adding these services, as the subcontracting process was working out so well and reducing their costs. However, Zelensky Brothers didn't have a clear competitive position, and so their sales force was incentivized in a way that encouraged employees to close new accounts and aggressive competition. There was no clearly defined competitive goal. His incentives indicated that he was trying to eliminate the competition when, in reality, he was trying to be mutually beneficial.

Due to the incentives, the sales force became vocally critical of the competition in the community. They disparaged the other companies' quality and service, often questioning their integrity. In other words, they did everything a sales force naturally does when they want to win and win big. As they continued this tactic, animosity started to build.

Big companies are often slow to respond to threats, but when they do, they bring a lot of force to a specific area. In retaliation, these competitors refocused their efforts in this regional location, restructuring their specialty services department to punish and limit their contractors from working with Zelensky Brothers through contractual incentives to "not" work with them.

As the contractors refused to work with them, Zelensky Brothers had to begin expanding into the areas they had neither the capital nor expertise to handle. This sudden need to expand destroyed their business model, which was the reason the brothers created the company in the first place.

By the end of the year, Zelensky Brothers Cleaning was forced to close as they had spent all of their excess capital attempting to expand and, in the process, providing subpar service and losing clients.

This story is unfortunately common in business today. An

improvement in a product or service drives the formation of a new business that can bring value to customers but also changes the competitive landscape, often unconsciously. Without an intentional plan for approaching the relationships with other providers and customers, there is often detrimental action that affects the overall mission of the new company.

SO WHAT IS COMPETITION?

According to Merriam-Webster, competition is defined as "the effort of two or more parties acting independently to secure the business of a third party by offering the most favorable terms." Another popular definition is "the act or process of trying to get or win something others are also trying to get or win." In that vein, I would define competition as an interaction in which individuals or populations seek to gain a preferential share of resources.

These are all accurate definitions, to be sure, but they only scratch the surface of what competition truly is.

Competition is an inherent state based on our biology, our psychological factors, and the environment in which we find ourselves. Competition is inside all of us—literally. It is built into our genetic code.

The previous definitions look at competition as a contest or a comparative analysis. Really, competition exists inside all of us whether we are conscious of it or not, which means it exists in our businesses, whether we've defined it or not. You might be one of the many people who read that and thought,

Well, in my business, I'm just trying to do a good job. I'm not competitive at all. You may believe that, but all the research says you are.

When you're in a contest, there's a strong chance you know you're in that contest, so you make conscious competitive decisions in response. However, there's also an inherent interaction between you and your environment, which by definition, has you trying to gain resources from that environment.

THE BIOLOGY CONCEPT

Competition is arguably the most important factor structuring the living world (if you buy into the Darwinian Theory of Evolution, that is). However, the degree of competitiveness in each person and situation varies.

From a biology standpoint, there's natural selection, where selective gene mutations that are best adapted to gather resources from the environment are the ones most likely to reproduce and survive.

From a business standpoint, the concept is surprisingly similar. Businesses need to interact with their environments, and the ones that are able to "gather" the most resources survive.

I know that many of you are reading this and thinking, *But I'm not competitive, Brad.* Actually, you are.

Scientists have identified a gene sequence that controls your competitive nature. This gene decides if you are a warrior or a worrier. If you don't think you're competitive, there's a good chance you have the worrier version. If you're highly competitive, you're a warrior. Both types have advantages and disadvantages. No matter which one you are, the gene will influence how you react to stressful stimuli and associate with higher levels of competitiveness.

The COVID-19 crisis distinctly highlighted the difference between warriors and worriers.

Warriors were found across the country in hospitals: ER doctors who were literally on the front lines, exposed to the virus every single day. Yet they didn't quit; they continued to show up for work, day after day. But they didn't stop there. When the vaccine came out, many of these ER doctors volunteered to give it to the people they considered more vulnerable, even though there were limited quantities.

Worriers could be seen staying in their homes, masking when they had to go out, disinfecting their groceries, and doing their best to stop the spread. However, worriers struggled to handle the stressful stimuli the same way as their warrior counterparts. Warriors ran into the fray, while hospitals saw a great resignation from worriers.

Yet, warriors can be overly competitive. You can see it in nature, in humans, and even in viruses. Some viruses try to live as a mutually beneficial life form as it infects your cells, but some over-exploit their resources, which results in the death of the host (i.e., you).

There are several examples in nature where an animal has

gone extinct because their genetic ability to exploit their resources was actually a detriment—they destroyed their own environment. (And that's not even considering humans' destruction of animals and environments.)

For instance, Haast's eagle in New Zealand. This type of eagle transformed over time to hunt a single type of flightless bird. However, when humans moved into the area in the 1300s, they hunted the eagle's prey to extinction within a few hundred years. The eagle failed to adapt and went extinct as well in a phenomenon known as co-extinction.

Another example is the lionfish, which is considered an invasive species in the Gulf. When they first arrived in the Gulf, they began eating everything. Biologists believed they were going to destroy their competition as well as eliminate a lot of the prey. Instead, they've adapted: their population has gone down, and their competitors have not.

Too often, we can become competitive to gain an advantage and push it past the point of benefit. There's a balance that needs to be achieved, so you don't compete your way past success and into failure.

There's a conventional view of competition that it is: (1) a choice, (2) generally beneficial, and (3) drives innovation and improvement. While all three can be true, there's a nuanced nature to competition that's important for you to understand.

Unmanaged competition can create unproductive conditions. Your choices influence how beneficial competition is for you and your company.

WORRIER VS. WARRIOR

One of the biggest advantages of the worrier gene is that having less of that purely competitive drive and more advantage to memory and attention type of tasks will make you less susceptible to over-exploiting your environmental resources and putting yourself into a negative situation.

As you think about putting your company team together, you want people who have the ability to be more cautious as opposed to the people who will drive that. It's how much risk you are willing to bear, or in this case, it's how much thought and attention you give to the interplay between you and your environment versus just the natural desire to dominate or exploit that environment.

Once you acknowledge the competitive aspect of business, the natural assumption is that everyone is always trying to eliminate or destroy the competition, when the reality is that there are several situations in which that's not the best thing to do. If your whole sales team is aggressive warriors (which they often are, as warriors make successful salespeople), they run the risk of harming your business position, just like we discussed at the beginning of the chapter.

Warriors can become so focused on winning every sale possible that they over dominate the resources or eliminate the competition so completely that they cease to exist when what they should have done was strike a balance and either isolate or find a way to work in a synergistic, mutually beneficial environment with your competition. With a team of warriors, you run the risk of ignoring potentially beneficial strategies and failing to maximize profit.

They'll win as far as they're concerned because they drove the competition out of business, but by doing so, you may be forced to take on lower profit business or business that you're otherwise not equipped to take. As in the case of the cleaning business, taking on these extra services could end up putting you out of business as well.

Worriers are genetically predisposed to be more risk-averse and be less driven by comparative analysis. A lot of times, these folks are probably your accountants, so they're looking at what makes money and what doesn't, where they have to invest expenses, and where they don't. In terms of phenotypic expression of the competition gene, you're going to see a tendency for your finance people to look more holistically at where your advantage lies.

It's important to remember, however, that the environment you put around your warriors and worriers can affect how they act and react. Again, looking back to our example chemical company, the owner had created a sales incentive, as many companies do, for new accounts—and that appeals to the warrior gene. So even if you are trying to hire a good mix of warriors and worriers, any sales incentives will attract more warriors to your team. After all, most people self-select themselves out of roles that we aren't comfortable with, especially if we don't have the right genotypic make-up for it. We go where we are most successful and avoid where we are uncomfortable.

Competition is inherent. We exist because of competition. Our world looks the way it does because competition led to genetic mutations and variations that were selectively enhanced by the availability of environmental resources.

CHAPTER TWO

FOUR MAIN PSYCHOLOGICAL FACTORS

In 2016, Wells Fargo faced a huge scandal.

Workers were being incentivized to sign up new customers. In fact, Wells Fargo published a rank order list of who was opening the highest number of new accounts, and if you were at the bottom of the list—you got fired.

Employees were so scared to be at the bottom of the list that they were incentivized to fraud. They were opening up fake checking accounts and fake credit card accounts for customers who never wanted them.

In the resulting trial, Wells Fargo claimed they were trying to control the situation. They said 5,300 employees were fired for sales misconduct—yet more than 8,500 were fired for performance issues, including failing to meet sales goals.

The company used incentives to attract employees to the company and then used rank order lists to keep them motivated. Essentially, they had both a carrot and a stick that led to a long court case, the company getting fined in the millions, and most of the executives, including the CEO, being fired.

Ranking and incentives are only two factors that can affect competition in employees. If you look into all the available literature on competition and the associated psychological factors, you'll find thousands of papers covering hundreds of factors. However, for me, it breaks down into four major categories, each of which has two subcategories that are particularly noteworthy from a business standpoint.

IDENTITY

The Axe deodorant brand's target market is young men. And in the US, they launched a series of ads that were very entertaining and successful. However, these same ads didn't work in Italy.

Unlike their US demographic, the young men they were targeting in Italy were still living at home with their parents. The identity of these men when they saw the TV commercials was not of a sexy, available young man because their parents were in the room. It was of a dutiful, nice, respectful son because any other type of behavior was uncomfortable in front of mom.

Axe specifically switched their tactic. They took the ads off TV, and instead, advertised on billboards that were set up where their audience was going to be at night when they were out with their friends. The men ate it up, and Axe sales skyrocketed.

These men had a different social identity depending on where they were—and your employees, your customers, your suppliers, everybody you deal with, has that same variability in their identity.

We all have a viewpoint of ourselves that drives our decision-making and thought process about ourselves, and it's malleable. In the Axe example, the viewpoint can be about how you view yourself in a specific moment, or it can be how you view yourself in a social group.

Let's look at another example using soccer (or football, depending on where you're living as you read this).

Researchers performed an experiment to see if fans would help an injured person. In the first stage, they had their actor dress in a Manchester United shirt and then "fall" down the stairs at a Manchester home game. Everyone nearby ran to help him. In the second stage, they had the same actor wear a Liverpool jersey at a Manchester home game and "fall" down the stairs again. This time, no one came to help. There was a social identity created simply by wearing a jersey, and the identity was so strong that people refused to help someone not in their group, even if they would have helped in any other situation outside of the stadium.

This is commonly seen in NFL games, too. If you wear a Raiders Jersey to a Chiefs game, you're most likely going to get in a fight. It seems ridiculous because those two people wouldn't otherwise get into a fight, especially over something as silly as a spilled drink or accidental shoulder bump, but that's the power of identity.

How we see ourselves as individuals and how we see ourselves as fitting into a group both have an immediately impactful effect on how we interact and, therefore, how we approach competition.

It's: "I don't want to hurt you, but if we put on different football uniforms and go out on the field, I'm gonna try to kill you." In fact, you're probably even going to be somewhat emotional about that. The best fighters try to keep emotions controlled, but they still have a competitive viewpoint of themselves, which is: "I need to kill you. I'm a killer." Then, as soon as the bell rings and the fight is over, they're hugging.

I bet you're thinking, *Well, yeah, Brad. Of course, they do that. It's the rules of the sport.* However, people do this *all the time*. It's not limited to sports (they're simply the most common example). Humans act in accordance with how they view themselves, and that view can be primed—easily.

Researchers have found that the message you give a participant before they go into an interaction will drastically color that interaction. Hundreds of studies have been done where researchers have pre-exposed people to specific stimuli and then watched their responses change based on the stimuli that they received ahead of that interaction.

Erie Chapman, former chief executive of Riverside Methodist Hospital, founding president of Nashville's Healing Trust, and founder of the Erie Chapman Foundation, wrote a book based on this idea of pre-exposing stimuli called *Radical Loving Care*.

While a hospital administrator in the eighties, he made sure that there was a religious or otherwise emotionally connecting symbol outside every hospital room. But it wasn't for the patients—it was for the staff. He knew it would change their behavior if he primed them to be thinking of themselves in a different light, and he was right. You're different if you're sitting in church: the identity that you form of yourself there is very different than it is if you're sitting in a bar or at a game. He found that caring behaviors were stimulated through priming.

Identity can be broken into two main subcategories: personal identity and social identity.

PERSONAL IDENTITY

People act in accordance with how they view themselves, but there's a catch. How you view yourself at any given moment depends on what you are doing and what you are focused on at that particular moment. If we have a long discussion focused on altruistic behavior, and then I put you into a decision-making arena, you're going to act in accordance with how you have now, at least in that moment, come to view yourself.

If you spend your time putting on a military uniform, loading your weapon, and training as a soldier, in that moment, you view yourself as a soldier. You're going to do what you know you're supposed to do from a personal standpoint.

In recent years, there has been an increased spotlight on police shootings. A common question is, "Why are cops shooting people when they shouldn't be?" The answer lies in personal identity. They shoot because they are acting in accordance with how they view themselves: "I'm the law; I'm the authority, and you need to listen to me. These are the tools that I have at my disposal to make that happen." Then when we watch the video on TV, we ask, "Oh my God, why would a human being ever do that? Why would you shoot somebody over a traffic stop?"

That police officer, for good or bad, is acting in accordance with how he views himself when he put that uniform on and assumed that role as a police officer. I'm not saying that he is right, wrong, or anything in between. I'm simply saying that his decision is based on his personal identity of being a police officer.

Years ago, I volunteered on the SWAT team as a medic. After the tragedy of 9/11, our department received a lot of money from Homeland Security. We already had some equipment, but after the windfall, we suddenly had all new, state-of-the-art military-grade equipment. We even received a bearcat, which is a bulletproof transport vehicle that you can drive up to the front door—it's essentially a tank on wheels. I can tell you first-hand that receiving all of this equipment can change your identity.

After we received this equipment, the team wasn't doing

regular police work anymore. Every time we were sent out, the team considered it a military mission. There was no fact-finding. It became: here's the house, here's how we're going to take it down, and everyone gets zip-tied first, questioned later. If they appeared to pose a threat, it was likely to elicit a violent response.

During the extremely short amount of time it took to take a house out, the team would act in accordance with how they viewed themselves in that moment, which was a militarized individual following orders. It showed me firsthand how soldiers can adopt a focused mentality and do things that are otherwise unthinkable—even to them. This is a powerful example of how, in the moment, your personal identity can so strongly influence your behavior.

We can all do that. This isn't limited to the police and military. Yes, most of us structure our lives so that we never have to experience those kinds of extremes, but sometimes you end up in a situation (say, immense pressure at work to hit sales figures).

Depending on the message you give your team, and how you set your competitive position (or worse, if you let it evolve on its own), people will act in accordance with their view of themselves while at work. This view can either help your company or destroy it if it's not set appropriately.

SOCIAL IDENTITY

Your social identity is a shared identity. It doesn't rely only on how you view yourself.

Let's reach back to the Manchester United experiment. Just by wearing a jersey, you have a social identity with a specific group of people. That identity gives you a natural tendency to compete against groups that are perceived to be outside the boundaries or antithetical to your group.

Politics is a great example of social identity. The United States has, essentially, a two-party system, and Trump exploited the social identity of Republicans. He has almost nothing to do with the population base that he's popular with, yet he's managed to create a common identity for these people as outsiders. Their common identity is stronger than voting in a direction that would be better for their actual needs. The power of that shared common identity that he's created is so strong that he's been able to polarize them: "You're with us or against us."

On the other side, Democrats have too many factions, which means they can't create a shared identity. As those factions become more extreme due to disagreements, the party continues to stop themselves from taking advantage of the power of social identity.

Once you are in a social group, it's difficult to leave. Let's go back to sports. Once a soccer fan picks a team, or a football fan picks a team, they stay by them through thick and thin. They never flip-flop to another team on a whim. There's an expectation around that identity that makes it challenging to leave the group once you're in.

RELATIONAL

There's the personal component of how we see ourselves as our identity, and there's how we see ourselves within the social group. Then there's the history we have with others and how that affects competition.

SIMILARITY

You may think it's strange, but the reality is that people are more competitive when they're compared to others that they feel similar to and less competitive when there are greater differences.

Think about your last family game night. You're naturally more competitive with your family than if you played with a group of strangers. However, as you get to know that group of strangers, even over the course of the evening, you may become more competitive as the monopoly game drags on, as it always does.

This applies across the board. From a business perspective, if you want to dissuade your employees from competition, you need to highlight any and all differences from your competition. However, if you want your employees to be competitive, you need to highlight the similarities to your competition—or create some if none exist. The more similarities you can find that get people to say, "Oh, these people really are a lot like me," the more likely you are to inspire competitive behavior.

Whereas if you say, "Well, we do some of the same things, but we're really a very different company. And here's why.

Here's how we're different," you can create differentiation and reduce the competitive feelings in your team. However, if you go too far in differentiating your company, you may be unintentionally telling your team that you're so different they aren't competing with them.

So, on one hand, as you try to create a social grouping with your employees, the more you can make your competition seem like them, the more likely they are to compete with them. On the other hand, the more different you set yourself up as, the more distinctive or dissimilar, then you're gonna have to build some competition back in. Both scenarios can be right for your company—you just need to think of what you are trying to accomplish when you're putting your incentives together.

RIVALRY

Rivalry is personal history and can obviously have a huge effect on both individuals or social groups. Again, the jersey: if, historically, you're a team fan and you have a rivalry with this other team, you're going to want to compete with, and even beat, them.

I always joke about college football. For the most part, the players are there for four or five years, and yet these colleges have long-standing, thirty- to forty-year rivalries. Well, none of those players experienced the start of that rivalry. They're in and out. Yet, they all talk about the rivalry. It's a historic relationship.

Rivalry has a huge relational impact on competitiveness.

Those teams get fired up for those games. There's even a rivalry week in college football. The colleges support these rivalries, partly because they sell tickets and partly because they encourage TV viewers. Colleges set up these things on purpose to help with sales and to get people to watch—it is part of their competitive position.

From a business perspective, you can imagine what an impact a personal history or narrative makes on how businesses have interacted with each other. If you've enjoyed a mutually beneficial existence for years, employees probably have a healthy competitive tone between them. Whereas, if you have been trying to drive each other out of business forever by undercutting and discrediting each other, your employees are going to have an unhealthy rivalry. In each business, every individual's identity will be affected dramatically by the historic relationship.

As much as you try to control the social identity of your company, how your employees view themselves and how you set up the similarities (or differences) between you and your competition, you have to respect what the relationship has been like historically.

If you have a rivalry with another company, is it friendly, or is it oppositional? If the latter, you need to acknowledge it and the effect it is certainly having on your employee's social and personal identities, as their competitive actions will be directly related to those identities. You can't ignore it. And if you want to change how competitive your employees are with your competition, you need to be aware of and address the history.

You see this a lot when Company A merges with Company B, and then, not long after, they split again, or Company B gets sold. Often they couldn't make the merger work because, historically, they had competed against each other or had developed a narrative of rivalry that they couldn't resolve even after coming together.

A real-life example is Geisinger, who merged with Hershey. At the time, it was a big deal. Hershey had a bigger medical school and more academic-type resources, while Geisinger had more of a clinical footprint. It was going to be a great marriage of learning and doing. However, the merger only lasted a few years before the two companies split again because the board decided it wasn't working.

Part of their merging failure was likely related to not appropriately recognizing and managing the historic rivalry. To do that, two or three years ahead of the merger, they needed to focus on redefining their historic relationship and rebuilding the personal and social grouping identities. They didn't, and so the merger didn't work.

INCENTIVES

The incentives you build into the structure of your company will drive competitive behavior. If there's a clear benefit to me achieving some advantage over you, then it's cause for me to act in ways that I might not otherwise. And that's from both a consumer standpoint and an employee standpoint.

DIRECT INCENTIVES

Direct incentives are when there's an obvious benefit to the actor to execute and achieve that incentive goal. Two examples of direct incentives for consumers to pick Company A over Company B are rebates and coupons.

The biggest example from an employee standpoint includes bonuses for things such as sales and production. Depending on how you structure your bonuses, you're going to drive certain forms of competitive behavior.

Think back to the story from Chapter One. The owner was incentivizing new customer acquisition—that's a direct incentive affecting the sales team's competitive behavior. Combine that with the right mix of identity and genetic makeup, and you've created a sales force that is very aggressive, which may or may not be good for your company.

Incentivizing your team is neither good nor bad. It's simply something you need to think about when you're structuring your incentive package. Bonusing based on an employee's margin on sales for the year versus paying for number of accounts closed are two very different incentives that will drastically change the competitive nature of your employees.

Hospitals can incentivize their physicians, for instance. As CMO, I directly incentivize my physicians to see patients and perform surgery by paying them on a Relative Value Unit Mechanism—whether the hospital gets paid or not. Essentially, they're directly incentivized to get patients in or steal patients, if they can, from other providers. It helps save the hospital money because the physicians don't want me to recruit more physicians as there's an obvious benefit to them staying busy with more patients. They'd rather be booked out for a year, even if it means more work, fitting in extra patients after hours, or being on call at night.

This is the standard compensation mechanism in corporate health care and simulates the nature of independent practice based on collections. It ensures physicians are productive and busy. It's the same as with a sales team: you have the same amount of back-office support whether a salesman is successful or not successful. I have the same amount of overhead and back-office support whether a physician is doing one surgery a day or eight. Having five physicians doing eight surgeries is better for my overhead than ten physicians doing four.

However, this only works because this is for a not-for-profit hospital, which changes how I incentivize my physicians. As CMO, I want them to be busy regardless of whether the patient can pay. For profit hospitals don't incentivize their physicians to be busy—they incentivize their physicians to be busy for paying cases.

This is both good and bad. The good is that this type of incentivization allows physicians to care for people, regardless of their ability to pay. On the other hand, if a hospital performs more services that lose money than gain, they'll go broke and close. Plus, the dynamic nature of overhead costs can shift suddenly and make incentives detrimental so that even currently profitable activities can become unprofitable. Changing incentives frequently could be disruptive to your workforce and need to be carefully considered in the long-term strategic plan.

ZERO-SUM GAME

Another incentive consideration is whether you are in a zero-sum game. Zero-sum is competing for limited resources. A zero-sum game is when there are limited resources available in a particular environment for multiple actors to compete for—if I get a bigger piece of the pie, your piece is naturally smaller.

Most employees look at their business as a zero-sum: "I have a limited amount of opportunity in this environment to capitalize on these resources."

Take franchises, for instance. They are often limited by geographic territory. They get a guaranteed market area, but there's still a boundary. Because they're limited from selling outside of that, it becomes a zero-sum game for them. If you have a local coffee shop, you're in a zero-sum game with any other coffee shop that comes into the area because there's a limit on the amount of coffee consumers will purchase in that particular area.

The more obvious the zero-sum nature of your environmental resources is—in other words, the limit on the pie—the harder people will naturally fight for a piece of that pie. You've looked into this with your own company through a market analysis.

Online companies broke free from the zero-sum game by removing their geographic limitations. Plus, by selling multiple products, they reduced their demographic limitations as well. The only limitation they faced was who was willing to get on a computer to order. While, in the beginning, that may have been a small number of people to feel like a zero-sum game, today it's not a limiting factor at all.

Geographic limitations are limiting for more than franchises. Service professionals such as plumbers would lose money if they had to drive six hours to a job and six hours back. Physicians, especially if they are not specialists, are limited by who will drive to their office for a check-up.

Demographic limitations can be gender, age, working vs. non-working, etc.

RANKING

Ranking is a form of direct comparative analysis. The two main factors we want to focus on are audience and number. With ranking, I'm comparing you directly to someone else by ordering you or putting you on a list.

Often, in business, it's called benchmarking, which includes setting and tracking KPIs (key performance indicators), targets, goals, incentives, etc. Incentives, in particular, are often based on rank. In today's business world, ranking has become a common way to compare ourselves to the competition.

AUDIENCE

When I say audience in terms of ranking, I mean the transparency and visibility of a rank list, which drives competition.

Think of college ranking lists. Many magazines and websites will put together a ranking system based on their own opinion, and yet people will look at it and decide whether or not to apply to that school based on the popularity of the list. When my son was choosing where to go for graduate school, he knew he wouldn't go to a school that wasn't ranked in the top twenty of schools in the United States. College rankings have become so important that colleges compete to get higher on the list.

If you're number five hundred on a website that has no traffic, you're not going to care. If you are at the bottom of the list in People Magazine, you're going to pay much more attention to that, and work hard to move up the list because of the visibility of the magazine.

Transparency and visibility inside a company are just as important as external visibility. Many companies will put up a comparative rank or list in the main hallway in order to draw attention to it. They're trying to get their audience—employees—to see where they rank and drive competitiveness.

Again, you need to watch what you are sending to your employees because you could be driving too much competition. But in some cases, you may want extra competition. For instance, safety: "It's been 20 days since the last accident." These types of signs are capitalizing on the audience concept of ranking. It draws attention from your audience, so they are thinking about what you want them to think about.

This is one area where you don't have to compete against an actual competitor—you can compete against yourself. The more transparent and visible the ranking is, the bigger deal you make of it, and that will affect how your employees engage in competitive behaviors. You need to ask yourself if publishing an internal ranking is in line with and supports your competitive position.

Too many businesses today don't ask themselves this question, partly because these types of lists are so common. It can be hard for business owners to stop and think, "Is this driving the kind of behavior I want it to drive?"

NUMBER

A great example of number-ranking is grade point averages for students and the effect that it has on them. Academic ranking does motivate some students, but it actually demotivates and alienates others. GPA only measures a small slice of intelligence. Once you expand your metrics to include mental health and motivation, you see that ranking grades doesn't help the student overall. Instead, it's the totality of engagement in school.

Researchers found that from grade five to grade twelve, engagement decreases from 74 percent to 34 percent. The biggest drop happens when students go from eighth grade to ninth grade, with another big drop when they enter high school.

The fewer competitors you have, the more your competitive behaviors will increase. The more competitors, the less competition. If you're ranked one hundred out of five hundred students, you won't be highly motivated to increase your ranking, but if you're in the top twenty? You're going to work extremely hard to increase that ranking.

This is seen in business as well. The few competitors you have will enhance the competitive behaviors of your employees. The more competitors, the less competition. If you're one of fifty companies in the market, you don't have as much desire to distinguish yourself.

However, if there is a leader in your market, that leader becomes *everyone's* main competitor. This can cause what's called horizontal hostility, which is when an alliance forms between competitors in order to target the leader. "I don't really like you because you're competing for the same business as me, but we have a larger enemy, so we should form a mutual, limited bond."

The four factors—identity, relational, incentive, and ranking—are controllable. First, you need to understand them, and then, you can consider them in relation to your competitive strategy. What changes can you make to influence your employees to take the type of competitive action you want them to take?

CHAPTER THREE

YOUR VIEW OF COMPETITORS...AND YOUR COMPETITORS' VIEW OF YOU

You may have noticed, I like to have a story for every topic we cover in this book. The story for Chapter Three is...there is no story. There's plenty of research and observations around the idea of competition, but there's nothing that speaks to a company's competitive position.

The previous chapter discussed internal employee competition and how you have to strike the right balance between internal competitiveness and your company's goals. As I researched for this book, I found a few paragraphs here and there on a few unknown blogs that essentially said, "Hey, you should pay attention to this." That's it. No actual research, no solid examples of what a competitive position is, and why it's so important to know your company's view of your competitors.

For the thousands and thousands of business articles out there that deal with competition and employees' views of competition, everything is related to the internal structure of competition amongst your employees rather than an external view of how your employees are educated on your competitive position and how that ties into your mission.

WHAT'S YOUR VIEW OF THE COMPETITION?

When I work with consulting clients, I ask them a series of questions to get the ball rolling:

- What is your mission statement?
- What's the history around your mission statement?
- What is the ultimate, ideal state of the company within the market?

From there, we can start getting more specific, starting with: are there any benefits to having other companies in your market? This is a great question to get you started thinking about the state of your business, specifically within your market, and how your competitors can add or detract from your contribution to the market.

Then we look at it from a consumer perspective. Is there a clear consumer benefit to competition in the market? Most clients immediately say yes, but in fact, it's not necessarily the case.

Healthcare is a classic example of more competition being worse. There's a limited amount of healthcare resources, and if you diffuse those amongst several companies who all only want to take the profitable range of services, you'll have no one left to handle the unprofitable, but essential, services. (We'll talk later about how to dump non-profitable services on your competitor to make them a valuable contribution to the market *for you*.)

In healthcare, there are a lot of new technological investments that require capital investment to be able to use, which means hospitals need some profit margin. If they don't have a mix of profitable and non-profitable services, they won't have the margin to be able to invest in these advanced services. For instance, my hospital recently invested in a new stroke treatment that was costly to purchase but can save lives. If there were two hospitals in town, I wouldn't have the profit margin to be able to purchase the equipment.

Or, I could purchase the equipment, but then I'd have to be concerned about putting all the capital into an investment for something that may be necessary and beneficial for the community but may not drive a profit margin that warrants its creation. I was able to use profits from our profitable service lines to fund the things that don't make money—a common tactic in healthcare. (Ironically, most of the life-saving treatments lose hospitals money, such as ICU care.)

WHO EXACTLY IS YOUR COMPETITOR?

Once you've considered your ultimate ideal state, the benefits of allowing other market participants (or threats), and whether there's a clear consumer benefit, the question becomes: does that resonate as an aspirational journey of significance for you and your team?

If so, is it reflected in your mission statement? Because that's what a mission statement should be: an aspirational journey of significance. And if not, it's time to retell your story.

While most employees probably wouldn't say that the company mission is constantly resonating in their ears, it's still influencing them because it's influencing the company: the board sets policy based on it, operational policies get set on board policy, incentives are set on the policies, and so on and so on. Even the company culture is set on the mission statement.

The mission statement directly affects everything in the company, and if it doesn't consider how you view and interact with the competition (your competitive position), then your entire company could be misled. Most people I work with realize during this conversation that they've never really thought about it.

Once you've considered how your mission statement interacts with your competitive position (or doesn't), it's time to look into your organization's competitive strategy. This involves asking yourself a series of questions.

- How does your company see the competition? Are they enemies, friends, or something in-between?

....

....

....

- Are there variable perceptions within your workforce about the competition, or is there consistency?

....

....

....

- What attitudes and actions have you and your workforce displayed towards your competition in the past?

....

....

....

- Have you ever been the victim of negative behavior?

....

....

....

- Have you ever instigated it? (Almost everyone says no, but I bet you probably have. We'll talk more about negative behaviors in Chapter Five.)

....

....

....

- What are your competitors' strengths?

....

....

....

- What are their weaknesses?

....

....

....

- Are they filling any gaps in the market that you are not?

....

....

....

- Who are their supporters?

....

....

....

- What risks do you face from that support?

....

....

....

- How does that support structure view your company?

....

....

....

- Do you have any policies or practices that discriminate against those supporters?

....

....

....

That last question is always a fun one because, again, it's not something people ever think about. Apple iPhones discriminate against people who prefer an app that works on Google. Most gaming systems don't have games that can cross platforms. Many programs that work on Apple computers don't work on Microsoft computers. All of these are a form of discrimination in order to secure market share.

One of the most important things to consider is what the perceptions within your organization are of your competition. You need to be in charge of that—or they'll form it on their own.

Employee perception directly ties back to your understanding of the ideal state of your company and your mission statement. You may say, "My employees are very aware of our mission." You may think that, but they can't be aware of your full mission if you aren't even aware of your competitive position. People will fill in and make their own position guided by the psychological factors we discussed previously and the guide rails you've put in (wittingly or unwittingly).

You can't control their position if you can't define it. Answering the questions in this chapter will help you define your position.

HOW DOES YOUR COMPETITIONS' VIEW OF YOU IMPACT YOUR COMPETITIVE POSITION?

Again, this is another self-awareness question. Ultimately what I'm asking is: what do you think your competition thinks of you? Because that's all you can really do. You're on one side of the equation with no real way to know the other side.

The first question to ask yourself is: do you know what your competition's mission is? Do you know what their goal is? For instance, do you truly believe their goal is to be the only offering in the market and eradicate you? Do you believe they're fully comfortable with their share of the market, and they're not looking to expand at all?

Have they mastered a particular area? For instance, if the best burger joint in town is right next door to where you want to build a McDonald's, you probably want to consider building elsewhere.

Depending on how you answer these questions, you may need to either change your competitive position or build in the best response to potential competitive tactics. (We'll go into competitive responses in Chapter Ten.)

If you don't know how your team views the competition and how they view you, you can't properly write your mission and purpose statement, which means nothing else downstream will be set up for success in your market. In fact, detrimental events will occur, such as competing yourself out of the market like in our chemical company example. Remember, competition is an inherent human state of being. It will manifest itself no matter what, so if you want it to work for you, you need to control it.

The answers to these questions will set you up to use the framework discussed in Parts Two and Three.

CHAPTER FOUR

POSITIVE COMPONENTS OF COMPETITION

In 1945, a doctor created a special surgery technique and wanted his patients to experience a higher level of service than the existing hospitals could provide—so he built his own. The Shouldice Hospital was established by Dr. Edward Earle Shouldice in Ontario, Canada.

The Shouldice Hospital is a specialty hospital that focuses only on one very particular type of surgery: hernias.

The hospital set out to be, and is to this day, the world's leading center of excellence in abdominal wall hernia repair. Their specially trained staff performs over 7,000 hernia repairs annually, and they have the lowest infection rate in the world. Dr. Shouldice's repair method uses the body's own natural muscular walls and tissues to reclose tears, rather than relying on artificial mesh. There is no other hospital that can compete with the success of this hospital.

Now, Dr. Shouldice probably never decided to be in competition with other hospitals. He started his hospital because he discovered a way of performing hernia repairs that was unique, and he wanted to be able to care for his patients at his speed and in his own way, which required building his hospital as a separate entity.

He was so successful that the level of service he pioneered is now referred to as the Shouldice experience. Today the hospital is a modern, eighty-nine-bed facility built on a country estate just a few minutes outside of downtown Toronto. They provide exceptional care, ultimate comfort, and convenience for the patient.

He may not have realized what he was doing, but Dr. Shouldice was choosing a mastery competitive position when he started his specialty hospital. And today, no one can compete with it. If you own any kind of surgery center or hospital where you do an array of procedures, you're not going to be as good as somebody who's chosen mastery as a goal.

The company that chooses mastery doesn't even need to really compete with you using any negative components, such as adversarial criticism of or discrediting, because there's no comparison between what you're offering. You have separated yourself from the pack so distantly that even though you are providing a similar service, you have set yourself up as being entirely different.

This is what mastery does. However, it required a huge upfront investment in resources and commitment, which is why so few people do it. Mastery is an example on the extreme end of what is considered a positive aspect of competition: you have an innovation that's coupled with service excellence not otherwise seen in that particular industry, creating a recipe for success.

The good news for you is that mastery is only one form of positive competitive position. Let's look at a few others.

WHAT DO YOU MEAN POSITIVE COMPONENTS?

Positive components are part of a spectrum of competitive behaviors that most people consider to be generally more positive.

For instance, one of the pros of competition can be that you increase the development of new and innovative solutions, focused expertise, and niched services. Plus, competition can typically drive down consumer costs and doesn't allow for price gouging (say, when a larger company buys up all the small pharmaceutical companies that happen to be the only manufacturer of a particular drug and then quadruples the price).

Competition allows for diversified opportunities with a market that will raise quality and lower prices. Pursuit of market share will cause an increase in the value to consumers.

Most people see competition as a negative thing, but it depends on the context in which you phrase it. Sure, done wrong, it can be bad (like if you're an ice skater and your boyfriend hits somebody in the knee), but generally, a free market system can bring positive attributes to consumers.

POSITIVE COMPONENTS

- **Expertise**
- **Innovation**
- **Price Lowering**

The components listed above are generally considered to be positive, but know there's no hard line on the spectrum of behavior between positive and negative. It's part of human nature to move up and down the spectrum, and unless you do so selectively and purposefully, it will evolve as a cultural element among your employees.

EXPERTISE

Expertise can be broken into two subsets: mastery and specialization.

One of the benefits of competition is driving expertise in a particular area, and mastery is one example of that. Mastery takes expertise to an extreme, such as in the Shouldice hernia hospital.

As another subset of expertise, specialization is the start of the journey towards mastery. Usually, specialization starts in a narrow, unique niche that grows and evolves into mastery. Specialization usually goes hand in hand with innovation, as it improves on current offerings to produce unique products that fit a particular customer need.

INNOVATION

Innovation is building a better mousetrap. When someone

has a product, a competitor can look to improve upon that product. Innovation is one of the most popular competitive components. It's affected most of the items we use in our daily life, such as our mobile phones and laptops.

PRICE LOWERING

Price lowering is a fundamental macroeconomic principle. The more competition you have in a market, the more the price will decrease. This is why many people want to break up monopolies. It's also why governments create antitrust laws.

Monopolies can charge whatever they want, but if they have competition, the consumer has a choice, and that will drive the cost to where it needs to be to provide service at the level of excellence the consumer wants.

CHAPTER FIVE

NEGATIVE COMPONENTS OF COMPETITION

Saul Alinsky was a community organizer who got his start in the late 1930s. His work culminated in a famous book that came out in 1972: *The Rules for Radicals*. In the book, Alinsky lists his thirteen rules for empowerment.

As a community organizer, he was focused on organizing the socioeconomically disadvantaged in fights against a power structure, such as the city or an abusive company. All of his rules roll up into the idea of looking for an external antagonist and villainizing them.

Of the wide range of possible human behaviors, Alinsky points out that you can use negative components of competition to "attack" these villains through means such as discrediting, threatening, and disrupting.

WHAT DO YOU MEAN NEGATIVE COMPONENTS?

These are all adversarial components. They are usually used to attack and take down your competition (or that your competition uses against you). You can purposefully choose to use these behaviors as Alinsky points out. But if they don't align with your mission statement or purpose, you need to make it a very clear part of your competitive strategy that they should *not* be used.

Every time I bring up negative components, people say, "I would never do anything negative." But the fact is, you do, even if it's as a counterattack. It's an unfortunate truth that it's human behavior to engage in these components. While some of them may take some thought and effort to set up, such as creating a lawsuit, others happen without much thought, like a casual comment to a potential customer about the shortcomings of your competitor to show how much better your company is. "I heard Brad was having supply chain issues."

These casual comments can add up, however, which is why, as a leader, you need to pay attention to the competitive strategies your employees use and how you incentivize them.

NEGATIVE COMPONENTS

- **Discredit**
- **Threaten**
- **Disrupt**

DISCREDIT

Any kind of rhetoric, whether that's direct advertising or behind-the-scenes efforts, that is used to lessen the value of a competitor in the eyes of the market is discrediting them.

For instance, if you're a local company and you're up against a national chain, you can discredit them by saying their money goes to another state while yours helps the community. You can paint them as a puppet of outside people who don't care about the people who live in the area.

THREATEN

Threaten is an obviously negative competitive component. "If you do this, we're going to do that," is a typical threatening comment. This is used to keep your competition from overstepping. Another example is, "I don't make these types of products, but if you move into this particular market that I run, I'll start making them." Alinsky once said that the threat of a thing is usually more terrifying than the thing itself, and I've found he was correct.

However, threatening doesn't need to be overt. This is usually seen through speculating. "I've stayed out of your market, but I could always start moving into it." and "If you don't perform the way I want you to, then I'll do it myself" are often used against independent subspecialists. Or, if you control the supply chain, you can threaten to restrict their access to necessary materials.

Legal actions are a common threatening tactic that can sometimes be looked at as very expensive advertising.

They can be used to limit a competitor's ability to work in a market, through copyright or patents to stop them from creating a specific product, through cease and desist actions, or by opening a dispute on purpose to add legitimacy to a company's claims. However, it's important to be careful with legal actions, as they can cast shadows on your company and can have significant ripples that affect your stock prices and investor confidence. Plus, outstanding claims can impact your company's valuation if you're looking to sell.

DISRUPTION

One of the best ways to cause disruption is by stealing a competitor's best employees. It's an increasingly common tactic today. It's been covered in a lot of articles in the 2020s due to the reduced number of talent and increased number of jobs.

Or, if you see talented employees at another company and you want to hurt that company, you may want to steal them away even if you don't necessarily want or need that person. They can benefit you with their knowledge, sure, but you also harm the competitor by removing that talent from them. This is very common with salespeople, as once they develop connections in a territory, they're worth a lot.

If Company A buys Company B, it's a common tactic for Company C to recruit Company B's best employees so that the value of Company B goes down after Company A has paid a lot of money for it.

Creating insignificance is another way to cause disruption that is commonly overlooked, but it's very interesting. You can think of it as behind-the-scenes, quiet discrediting. In some ways, creating insignificance is one of the most violent things you can do, yet it's done with a really soft knife.

Often used by politicians, if someone has a particular role or status, you can remove their status or reduce their role to give yourself an advantage over them. For instance, politicians losing committee appointments because they went against party leadership. The leadership then creates insignificance by removing them from a powerful committee.

Creating insignificance is one of the most damaging competitive tactics and the hardest to counter because by the time you've made someone insignificant, it's too late for them to be able to counter—they've lost their voice.

It's also a tactic used when you want to purchase a competitor. You want to devalue them first so that you can buy them for less, but you don't want to discredit them so much that you eliminate the organization. You can make the leadership or board feel insignificant, so they feel like they have no other choice but to sell, and you're more likely to get a better deal financially.

PART TWO

THE STRATEGIES

Part One covered why competition is important. Now it's time to discuss how to approach competition in my company. To help, we'll look at the three strategies you can build your framework on: elimination, isolation, or mutual benefit.

CHAPTER SIX

ERADICATION

Trump's 2016 and 2020 campaigns are both remarkable examples of how to completely destroy your competition. While these days, almost every political campaign has elimination as its goal, Trump took this to a fantastic level.

If you look at any video from any of his campaign stops, you'll see Trump being hypercritical and insulting of anyone who he was competing against, whether they were in his own party or not. In the past, many people would have said, "There goes someone who's burning their bridges. You're not going to see any of these people on his cabinet or supporting him."

Especially in the 2016 primaries, most people thought that after each opponent was knocked out of the race, they would have merged together and decided to support another candidate. Yet, every time he managed to get them to support him, instead, even as he continued to criticize the remaining opponents (and sometimes the people supporting him!).

Trump is a clear example of using negative or adversarial components as part of his competitive strategy. He didn't focus on what he was going to do once in office or any innovations or improvements he was going to bring, which is what most of the other candidates did. Traditionally, there's an 80/20 focus: 80 percent of the talk is focused on what you will do for the voters, while 20 percent is discrediting the competition. Trump, however, abandoned that playbook. He didn't even try: "I have a great plan. It's going to be terrific." And then he would launch into negative talk.

This type of tactic is only used when your goal is to eradicate your competition. None of the tactics Trump used are used when you expect to have a positive relationship with the competition in the future.

WHAT IS ERADICATION?

When you choose eradication as your competitive strategy, you are deciding that it's in your best interest for your competition to not exist. When you eradicate a competitor, you can make it so they simply no longer exist in the market at all or that you acquire them, and therefore, they become you. In either case, they cease to exist.

Before you decide to go the eradication route, you need to ask yourself a few questions. The first and most important being: do you rely on your competitor for anything? If you answered the questions back in Chapter Three, you should have an answer to this question, which will tell you if it's really in your best interest to destroy your competitor. Do they serve a component of the market that you can't serve for some reason? If so, by eliminating them, you may be opening the door for five other companies, or maybe one huge company, to come in and push *you* out.

Yet many people believe that the ultimate goal of any business is to eliminate their competitors. But think about boxers. Two "rival" boxers can make millions fighting each other. Sometimes it's in their best interest to lose a fight because they can make even more on a rematch. In this case, eradicating the enemy—making it so they can't fight for some reason—is not in the boxer's best interest.

So even if your first instinct is to say that you want to eliminate the competition, you need to make sure of it first, because you may be in a mutually beneficial relationship, like the boxers. Consider all of the ramifications before you begin an eradication strategy.

Spending all of your effort and energy to eliminate someone may end up costing you something that you don't expect. One of the primary means of eliminating competition is to cut prices because you assume you can sustain losses longer than your competition or that you can be more efficient with a narrower profit margin until they are eliminated.

But again, that may not be a smart thing to do because you may not be able to reset product price expectations, meaning you may end up stuck at your new lower prices going forward. You can't cut your rates for a year or two, watch the competition go out of business, and then expect to get your old rates back. Consumers will not react well, and you may go out of business yourself.

ELIMINATION

If you decide you are better off without them—you can fulfill all the needs, there are no supply chain issues that require their existence, there are no service or product needs from them in the community—then it's time to eliminate them from the market. "There can only be one."

A classic example is Facebook versus MySpace. MySpace had every advantage: they were first in the market, they had a lot of value, they had professional management, they had big business backing, so they had all the financial resources they could need. Then here comes Facebook, started by under-grads. It probably didn't even seem like competition at first.

Facebook competed through innovation—from the positive end of the spectrum—and by having a key difference, which was allowing the customer to design the platform for what they wanted. MySpace, on the other hand, had already entered into the corporate pitfall of trying to tell consumers what they wanted. In the end, Facebook eliminated them simply by being extremely aggressive with their platform's innovation.

Another example is Netflix versus Blockbuster. Blockbuster, for those of you who may be younger, was a physical store you would go to and rent VHSs and DVDs. If you didn't return your rental on time, you'd get charged a late fee. The last time I went to a Blockbuster, I was returning a movie, and there was a big line, so I started wandering around the store. Once the line went down, I went up to the counter to return my movie, and the clerk said, "This is late." I was surprised since they were due back that day. She continued, "They were supposed to be returned by 3:00." It was 3:10.

"There was a line. You saw me here, in the store."

"Well, I still have to charge you."

I paid, and I never went back to Blockbuster. And I'm not the only one who hated the late charges. They were often crucified for them. Netflix, when they first came on the scene, also rented DVDs, but they did them via mail order. While their late fees were just as punitive, you weren't chastised in public for being late. And if you never returned the movie? They just billed you a fee, and that was it.

The other thing Netflix did was get on the forefront of digital streaming. It was a huge innovation that you may have noticed has changed the entertainment industry. Netflix never had to engage in any negative components because Blockbuster did it themselves with their late fee scandals.

Both of these examples show that just because you want to eliminate your competition, you don't have to use brutal, negative components like Trump did. Instead, you can use positive traits like out-innovating them or providing better service.

You can also eliminate your competition through price wars. Walmart is a great example of this. They moved into medium-sized towns across the country, set their prices low, offered a wider selection, and wiped out all of the small-town businesses. But they didn't just eliminate local competition—they were able to use this tactic to drive Kmart into bankruptcy as well. Walmart managed their supply chain and company very carefully, eliminated waste, and increased efficiency in order to lower their prices, and Kmart was unable to compete.

Walmart was about to take Rubbermaid out as well. In order to reduce prices to consumers, Walmart would pressure their suppliers. They would tell suppliers how many of their products they sold the year before and then tell them they need a lower wholesale price in order to continue selling their products. In 1996, Rubbermaid thought they had enough brand recognition to stand up to the big bad chain store, so they refused. Walmart followed through on their threat and cut Rubbermaid products from their store. Rubbermaid wasn't able to handle the loss, and within a few years, they were acquired by another company for a steal.

This example shows that price wars don't have to happen on the consumer end. It can be putting pressure on suppliers. Whether the company then passes the savings on to the consumer is up to them.

ACQUISITION

You don't have to force a company to go out of business to eliminate them. Instead, you can acquire them—that way they're no longer the competition, because they're you. You can either fold them in completely, or it can be a merger where they keep some control and minimal identity.

Rubbermaid, for example, changed hands, but their name was big enough that the acquiring company, who you've probably never heard of, decided to keep it. That's why you can still buy Rubbermaid products today. It's just not the same Rubbermaid that your parents bought. The company ceased to exist as a competitive entity, and now it exists as a shared bottom line.

American Airlines' acquisition of US Airways is another great example. In 2013, US Airways was having financial issues, and then the union issues began. American Airlines, on the other hand, had better relations with those unions, and as a result of the combination of factors, they were able to acquire US Airways. Unlike Rubbermaid, however, they did not keep the name and, instead, became one business under American Airlines.

Questcor is another fascinating story. In the late 1990s and early 2000s, it was common to see a pharmaceutical company, particularly one with a monopolistic corner of a market, buy up potential competitors so they could shelf their products. That's exactly what Questcor did. They bought a drug that treated Addison's disease from Novartis for $135 million—which they promptly shelved. They also bought a startup company.

This new company had designed a drug that treated immune-related disorders, and that would sell for a few hundred dollars a vial. This drug treated the same issue as a drug Questcor created that was selling for $8,000 a vial. Because Questcor had the market cornered, they didn't want this startup coming in and creating a price war.

While buying a drug that would be an innovation because it can be manufactured and sold much cheaper would be on the positive end of the spectrum, shelving it to continue selling your extremely expensive drug with a higher profit margin could be considered on the negative end (if you're a consumer; if you're a shareholder, it's brilliant).

CHOOSING ERADICATION

If you've decided that it's in your best interest to eradicate the competition, either through elimination or acquisition, you need to ask yourself if you can service the entire market and not risk another company coming in and creating a bigger problem than you had to start with. If you want to eliminate through innovation, do you truly have an innovation that's capable of being a Netflix- or Facebook-style disruption? Is your innovation easy to copy and, therefore, able to be used against you?

Make sure you think through every angle of your eradication strategy, so you don't have any negative kickbacks—and make sure it fits in with your mission and purpose. Does your plan fit with your values?

CHAPTER SEVEN

ISOLATION

WASA Papers was a poorly performing manufacturer of uncoated paper that had outdated machines and high production costs. However, what it did have was an unusually large share of the paper business in Chicago. When the new president of the company came on board and learned this, he began asking questions.

What he found was that WASA happened to have a factory close enough to Chicago that they were able to service their distributor daily. A light bulb went off, and the new president made this their new strategy. While they continued to sell traditional commodity products, WASA also began offering next-day service to all of their distributors located in major Midwestern cities. They encouraged their customers to order small, but more frequent, quantities and even place custom orders—and it worked.

WASA's customer base increased drastically, and because their customers were placing smaller custom orders, the company was able to charge premium prices. However, the president wanted to lock up the customers before any other company figured out what they were doing, so he released to the press that they had increased the speed of their deliveries by having larger inventory and working more—both of which were true, but they didn't indicate that they had done this through a major shift in strategy.

The strategy was to capture high-margin specialty products, and over time, they let their lower profit margin products, the commodity products, be sold to distributors by their competitors. This enabled them to put all their resources into their high-profit products. By the time their competitors realized what WASA was doing, they didn't want to get into small, costly product runs that came with immediate delivery expectations.

WASA took what had been an established market, redistributed it, isolated the competition to low-profit services, and cornered the high-margin speciality with an innovation they created. They realized it was better for their bottom line to let their competitors take services off their plate. The only reason they continued offering traditional products at first was so that the competition felt like they were outdoing them by getting contracts and didn't realize WASA was building this whole new business.

They used an isolation tactic to content their competitor to a portion of the market they didn't want anymore.

WHAT IS ISOLATION?

When the US military failed to eliminate the Taliban, they changed tactics and instead isolated the group in the mountains, holding the cities, towns, and infrastructure. Isolation is when you create a situation where the competition is tolerated and unable to get an advantage over you. There may be a benefit to having them in the market, but it's not a mutually beneficial existence (which we'll talk about in the next chapter)—the benefit is all yours.

Isolation is not an intuitive strategy. People naturally think of eliminating their competition, as we've discussed, and even the idea of striking a mutually beneficial deal with competition isn't far-fetched. But isolation in business isn't the first tactic that comes to mind (though it is a very common military tactic).

With isolation, the competition exists, but they can't grow or move into a new space. There are two main isolation strategies you can follow: contain or counter.

CONTAIN

When you contain, oftentimes, you are looking to match your competition. In essence, it's "me too": you're supplying a similar product, quality, or level of service.

When you're looking to isolate a competitor through containing, you are going to make sure that you have a viable alternative product or service so that competitor doesn't have the only presence in the market. Typically this is seen with companies that have other lines of business, but they don't have the expertise or financial resources to push others out of that market. What they can do is make sure that their competitors can't push them out of the market, as allowing the competition to have that entire market could be detrimental to your other main lines of business.

Think back to WASA. They had to decide if they were going to completely stop offering the traditional services, but they knew that if they did, it could hurt them. They didn't want to be known as the only paper company that couldn't serve all of their customers' needs.

Contain is best used when you need the market presence for the rest of your book of business, but eradication is on the table and you don't have a mutually beneficial partnership. When you choose a contain strategy, you need to decide what percentage of the market you are comfortable with having, whether that's 5 percent, 10 percent, or even 20 percent, so you can still advertise yourself as a full-service company.

A great example of contain is Honest Tea. They had great brand recognition, and they were available in multiple grocery stores. One day, Safeway, a grocery chain, approached them to produce a private-label brand to sell in their stores. This would mean that Honest Tea would be competing against themselves, which on its face didn't make sense.

However, the reality was that if they said no, Safeway would approach another company to produce the label. So either way, Honest Tea would have new competition. By accepting the contract, which they did, they were able to make additional wholesale profit off the new private label while also protecting their more popular and sought-after flavors.

Honest Tea contained their competition by competing with themselves. They stayed on the shelf in Safeway stores and protected their most popular flavors, which they only released under their Honest Tea brand. They also didn't have to try to counter their competition by beating the quality of a new private label. They couldn't eliminate the competition because they would be hurting themselves, and they couldn't do a mutually beneficial partnership by co-branding Honest Tea/Safeway because they'd offend all their other grocery store customers. An isolation strategy was the best competitive position they could choose as they were able to isolate and contain the private label's growth.

COUNTER

WASA is a great example of the counter strategy. They came up with and created a new segment of their market that allowed their competition to exist, but be unable to grow or compete in their new segment.

Counter, like contain, comes down to how much effort you are willing to put into your tactics. If you're a counter strategy, you may be willing to align with a credible partner against another competitor, which you may not be willing to do if you were only trying to contain them.

For example, if there's a specific niche area of business that you don't have, but a national chain or other company in the country excels in, and you want to counter your competition but don't have the resources to do so yourself, you can align with this credible partner to help shift business in your direction.

There are also negative components you use to counter. Even though you don't want your competition to be eliminated, you can still use threatening or disruptive actions to keep them siloed in their area—tactics you might not want to use if you were simply trying to contain them. If your values and mission don't align with negative tactics, however, you can use positive components instead.

Again, if you were trying to contain, you may not want to gain an innovative advantage over them, so you won't pour a lot of money into R&D to become more unique or highly visible. However, if you're countering the competition, you need to consider all of these tactics in order to counter their presence in the market and increase your market share. You'll want to appear more innovative, provide a better service, and/or have a lower price.

You can also isolate your competitors by recruiting their talent. By stealing their expertise, you can gain their advantage and make it your own.

An example of countering is from Baja Auto, which was a scooter manufacturer located in India. Scooters are a huge form of transportation in India, and Honda decided to enter the market. This posed a problem for Baja Auto because Honda was a bigger company with more tech. They couldn't stop Honda from coming into the market, and there was no way to eliminate them. Plus, Honda had a partnership with a local manufacturer, so they were able to not only sell the scooters but own certain components of the manufacturing process. Baja couldn't partner with Honda because Honda already had a partnership.

Baja Auto responded by looking at the advantages Honda was bringing to the market and at what advantage Baja had as a regional brand with their local recognition and distribution network. The only option they had was to isolate using a countermeasure. Baja Auto poured money into their product development. They looked into every one of Honda's technological advantages and outdid them.

The result was that Baja Auto's scooters got much better: higher tech, more bells and whistles, and more options. When Honda came into the market a few months later, Baja was able to hold them to an 11 percent market share. Honda never gained a big footing in India because Baja used their advantages, such as brand recognition and a large distribution network, and then increased and innovated on their offerings. They also reinvigorated their network: they visited every contact they had and ensured they were aware of all of the R&D Baja was investing in so they would want to get the new scooters right away.

Within a few years, Honda gave up and left the country.

CHOOSING ISOLATION

Imagine you have a knife company that makes all different kinds of knives, except steak knives. That wouldn't make a lot of sense to consumers. So, even if you are known for your cooking knives, and there are other companies that have the majority of the market on steak knives specifically, you should still offer a steak knife as well in order to contain your competition's share of the market.

If you are trying to contain your competition, you don't have to put a lot of effort into your steak knives. Simply having them is enough. But if you want to counter them, you'll need to put effort into your tactics.

This is where I see a lot of mistakes by my clients. They pick components of different strategies and then put money and resources into tactics that they wouldn't do if they had a clear directive on their competitive position. Why pour money into R&D to create an innovation in an area of the market that doesn't even align with your mission?

This is also where it's important to make sure your employees understand your competitive position. The person in charge of your steak knife department may not be happy with the idea of staying at 15 percent of the market and not improving their reach. They'll constantly be asking for resources and support to grow—unless they understand the bigger picture of how the company is positioning itself in the market and using contain strategies only, instead of counter strategies. And if you don't make an active decision to only use contain strategies, your employees will make a passive one. You'll see a range of behaviors all across the spectrum, even from yourself.

Isolation is a great choice of strategy if you think you may want a mutually beneficial relationship with your competition in the future. If you try to erase them off the face of the earth, they're not going to want to help you in the future. However, if you have a "you stay in your corner, and I'll stay in mine" strategy, they may be willing to work with you to increase both of your bottom lines. Eradication burns bridges; isolation keeps them minimally maintained.

CHAPTER EIGHT

MUTUAL BENEFIT

In 1997, Apple was on the brink of bankruptcy. They had invested heavily in R&D, but their sales hadn't caught up yet. They had increased their distribution network, and they had invested in their ecosystem. They needed more time for the improvements to turn into dollars.

Steve Jobs refused to let his company go under, so he swallowed his pride and called Bill Gates. Microsoft was the biggest software developer at the time, so they had plenty of money to spare. During their conversation, Jobs pitched why, even though they were in competition, Gates should bail out Apple. Gates agreed and invested $150 million into Apple, saving them. Today, they're worth almost a trillion dollars.

This deal was mutually beneficial for both Apple and Microsoft. Before the deal, there was no cross between Microsoft software and Apple computers. After the deal, there were Microsoft products being developed to work with the Apple ecosystem. Gates knew that Apple computers were more user-friendly, so even though they were competing on the hardware side, if he could open up the software side, he could make a lot of money. (He was right.) At the time, Apple also had a large lawsuit against Microsoft, accusing them of copying their operating system. Because of the deal, Apple dropped the lawsuit.

The benefit to Apple? They stayed in business.

WHAT IS MUTUAL BENEFIT?

Mutual benefit exists when there are clear benefits to both sides and a lack of imbalance that would lead to risk, in what I like to call a win-win incentive. In essence, there is mutually assured destruction. If we have the same amount of nuclear missiles, then we feel like we're balanced. If you have twice as many as me, then I'll feel like there's a risk.

In business, it's the same way. If one party is more powerful or has more resources, it can make the other party more cautious. After all, if the more powerful party changes their mind down the road, the smaller party would suffer. There need to be benefits for both sides and a lack of imbalance for a mutually beneficial strategy to work.

Mutual benefit is on the opposite side of the spectrum from elimination, of course. If you're working with someone, you're not going to want your people to do anything that could harm them. However, if you don't have a clear competitive strategy and your sales incentives are set up wrong, you may actually be incentivizing behavior that can hurt both sides of the partnership.

You also need to think about any history with a competitor that you want to enter a mutually beneficial relationship with. If your history is antagonistic, you need to ensure your employees understand that you're now friends. That's a good general business tip: today's competitor could always be tomorrow's partner, so always be careful with your competitive strategy. If you discredit a competitor, you'll eliminate the possibility of entering a partnership that could help or save you in the future.

You should also consider your areas of interdependence. Do you need them, or do they need you? What is the cost of matching their specialty? This reaches back to the questions you answered in Chapter Three. You need to know who your competition is before you get into a partnership to ensure you know what's a mutual benefit and what's a potential risk in disguise.

If you're dependent on someone for a raw material to make your product, but you both make that final product, that's a major risk for you. If they cut you off from that raw material, you're out of business, and they're fine. If you want to get a mutually beneficial deal off the ground, they would have to offer equity in the supply source or other shared resources so you can feel safe enough to enter into a deal with them (or vice versa). Ask yourself if any areas of interdependence are positives—or are they potential risks?

Once you answer all of these questions, you can decide which type of mutual benefit strategy you want to use: selective or complementary.

MARKET DOMINANCE

With a market dominance strategy, you are going to partner with a competitor in a specific area (not across the entire range of products) in order to keep others out of the market. (The Justice Department is often trying to stop companies from doing this.)

A great example is Amazon Marketplace. Amazon has a fulfillment service where they let third parties sell on Amazon's online store, and in return, Amazon receives a portion of the profit from each sale because they're acting as the fulfillment service. Both companies benefit, and yet Amazon is also able to keep other fulfillment companies out of the market.

Amazon considered what they already did well: sell products directly to consumers. But they were buying wholesale and selling retail, which meant they had to build a fulfillment department for their own products. Because they already had this service built, they realized they could selectively partner with other companies (or hundreds of thousands today). Amazon isn't partnering with these companies on their own products. Instead, it's a selective use of the fulfillment business to have a mutually beneficial relationship with other companies that could be competitors and, instead, bring in a small amount of profit. So when the competitors do well, so does Amazon, and the competitors get the benefit of Amazon's reach.

EFFICIENCY

Efficiency is when two companies are working together

in a way that increases value but decreases costs, usually through complementary technologies or products. Often they are working together to make a more complete set of products or services that fit in the same niche. With this strategy, you are working together in a specific area in order to save money, but still compete with each other on other products or services.

An easy way to think of it is ABCD: you do A and D, I do B and C, and together, we can make ABCD.

Car companies enter complementary partnerships all the time. Have you ever looked at a new lineup of cars across multiple brands and thought, "Wow, the entire body and look is similar to this other car brand"? That's because it is.

Car manufacturers often partner together to decrease the cost of manufacturing in the supply chain. Because of these partnerships, you'll see three different cars by three different brands that all use the same parts. However, the brands generally only work together on a particular body shape or type of vehicle, such as an SUV, in order to share the upfront costs. Outside of this partnership, they are competitors.

In 2013, Ford and GM agreed to share their transmission technologies. At the time, they both had different technologies, and instead of each company spending ridiculous amounts of money trying to rebuild each other's technologies, they decided to save money and share their innovations. This freed up their engineers to work on the next generation of vehicles (mostly electric ones) to compete with each other and other car makers. They knew it didn't make sense to spend time and money competing on a technology that was going to be outdated in a few years.

CHOOSING MUTUAL BENEFIT

Unlike the strategies under eradication and isolation, the two mutual benefit strategies aren't dissimilar. They aren't opposite strategies. Just like their main category, they are two elements that work together for the greater good.

When you choose to use a mutual benefit strategy, you need to be careful of how you set it up with your team. Steve Jobs had a Type A personality and was known to be, frankly, a jerk, so the assumption from employees was that he wanted an aggressive form of competition. Then, suddenly, he was having coffee with their biggest competitor and letting Gates buy into the company after years of Jobs telling them to hate Microsoft.

If you've never considered your competitive strategy before, and now you want to actively change it, know that shifting the mindset of your team can be difficult and will require time. Be sure to take your historic competitive tactics, whether they were by design or evolution, into consideration and create a change management plan.

And if you think you want to choose a mutual benefit strategy, be sure you understand the areas of strength and cost of supplementing weaknesses for each party before making a decision. Then, gain clarity around each side's strength of commitment to the agreement.

PART THREE

THE FRAMEWORK

CHAPTER NINE

CREATING YOUR OWN COMPETITIVE PLAN

Competition exists, whether you think about it or not. And depending on your business, it may have never been discussed. For physicians, it certainly isn't. We spend our time on anatomy, physiology, pathology, diagnostics, and disease treatment. There's no business education baked into medical school or residency. In fact, culturally, the idea of competition between physicians is abhorrent. The idea is that we're here to take care of patients and work together: "There are plenty of patients to go around."

That's true for general medicine, but when you get into niches, specialties, and geographic locations, you learn that there's differentiation in levels of profitability among different types of care, surgeries, and medical interventions. Suddenly you're out of med school, and you have to learn how to manage. You can't run a practice doing only things that don't generate revenue—your doors won't stay open long.

Because of this, the more profitable procedures become more competitive. There's a reason you see specific types of consumer-driven centers owned by physicians but not others. You won't see freestanding ICUs popping up because they don't make money, but you do see plenty of plastic surgery offices, vein centers, and orthopedic centers—all things that have a high reimbursement rate that can drive more expansion, which in turn creates a more competitive environment.

But this isn't talked about. Most people don't have a good framework on how to tackle competition or how to weave it into their business plan. Instead, it becomes a hole in their strategic plan. Instead of creating a competitive plan, they have business survival. They're copying what they see others doing and hoping it works.

The more I explored the idea of competition, the clearer it became that competition is inherent and has predictable behaviors and manifestations. I started to think, *These are things that ought to be controlled, but we can't control them if we don't know they exist.* I was in this place myself with no framework to work with. Over the years, my desire to categorize and simplify things from a diagnostic standpoint led to my need to create a treatment process (or framework) around the topic of competition. After a few years of research, I created a thought process, which led to a framework that can be weaved into existing business strategy.

BEFORE YOU CREATE YOUR COMPETITIVE PLAN

There are two essential components that you have to define for every business. They're the same thing you need to think about if you are interviewing for a job. The first is who we are, meaning the culture and mission of a company, and the second is how we do things. Your competitive position is a vital part of both of those components.

And yet, when you've interviewed for jobs, their competitive position never came up. They probably shared their mission statement and values—all businesses have them—and depending on what position you were applying for, you spent more or less time on them. Plus, some companies are just better at focusing on these things.

Take lululemon, for example. They are known for getting their new hires to focus on their mission, vision, and values—and they've come up with a brilliant way of incorporating individual goals into company goals. Every new hire writes their personal goal on a giant board: "I want to become a yoga teacher." And because the company incorporates your goals with theirs, it means you want to achieve their goals, as that will help you achieve yours.

And yet, even lululemon doesn't clearly define who their competition is, what their response is to competition, and what they want you, as an employee, to know and embrace about their competitive position.

In fact, very few companies do this. But, as we've said time and again in his book, if you don't define your competitive position, it will define itself based on the nature of your company, how you set up your incentives, the genetics of your employees, the social and historical identities of your team, and all of the other components we've discussed.

CREATING YOUR COMPETITIVE PLAN

First, define your ultimate state of your company within the market. Is it to own 100 percent of the market? To own all components of the production cycle? To own the supply chain leading to the production cycle? Before you do anything else, you need to be able to define exactly what it is your company is looking to accomplish.

I've found through my work that the higher up the position in a company, the more comprehensive answers I'll get to those questions. The lower down you go, the more vague and fuzzy the answers get—if they have any at all.

Next, ensure that your ultimate state definition resonates as an aspirational journey of significance within your mission and vision statements. This ultimate state is the base of your competitive plan. If it doesn't tie in with your purpose, you know that you need to begin intentionally managing that competitive plan (or update your mission statement).

Then, answer the following: how does all of this tie into the history that you tell of your company? Would everyone in your company tell you the same story? What about your customers? This begins to get into brand management. If you don't have a clear competitive position, then you don't have a clear mission statement and vision, and therefore, you don't have a clear story. Most likely, your employees will all have different stories depending on their level in the company, their department, and their history within the company.

Next, look at your incentives. Are you incentivizing your employees in a way that matches your mission statement?

Take a look at all of your answers to the above quotations. Do they match?

If they match, the question becomes: is our competitive plan working? Are we on the right track to achieve the ultimate ideal state of the company? If not, plan what changes you want to make. Review your answers to all of the questions asked so far and see if there are any foggy areas you need to clarify to improve your plan or if you need to change your strategy to better fit your goals. If yes, you're well ahead of the curve—congratulations!

If they don't match, then you have the opportunity to make them match! Use your answers to gain clarity around what you're currently doing versus what you want to be doing. If your competitive position doesn't match your clarity of purpose, look at what you need to change. It may be that your mission statement needs to be reviewed and tweaked to include your competitive plan, or maybe it requires a complete rewrite. However, most likely, your purpose is clear, but your competitive incentives and strategies don't match.

At this point, you have your mission statement, your purpose, and your competitive statement. You know all three aren't in alignment, so what should you do? Start by reviewing your answers to the questions in Chapter Three:

- Who is your competition?
- How do you view them?
- What is your relationship with them?
- How do they see you?
- Are there interdependencies?

Make sure you know how your entire team views the competition, too. They may have a different view of them than you do. From there, you can create a new competitive statement that aligns with your mission and purpose. You may find by revisiting the questions about your competition that you have been trying to eradicate them, but you have too many interdependencies, so you need to look at either creating a partnership or isolating them instead.

While you rewrite your competitive position, make a list of the tactics you want to do, depending on the strategy you have chosen. Once you finalize your strategy, you can review all of your current incentives. Do they match up with your new strategy? If not, it's time to make a plan to change them.

Next, it's time to execute the new plan, which comes with its own set of challenges. Before you announce your plan to your team, make sure you get buy-in from stakeholders. Don't just have your historic enemy appear on stage at a leadership conference to announce that he's buying into the company. Try to be more strategic and intentional with any change announcements (at least send a memo out beforehand, so the expectation is that they politely clap instead of shocking them and having them react with anger and booze).

One tactic I've used is to draw little stick people on the board as I list out my stakeholders, define them as groups (the board, executives, employee groups, consumers) or individuals, and then list out what their perspective is based on the current history. Then I ask myself if we switch gears from the current state to the ideal future state, how are each of these groups (or persons) going to be affected? How will their perception change?

Maybe customers will see this potential partnership as a bad thing because they're afraid prices will increase. That's a risk we'll need to address. How can we alleviate their concerns around that? Maybe you can offer a price reduction strategy to mitigate the risk and show customers that this is going to be a good change.

Once your stakeholders are on board, consider how you are going to roll this out to your staff. Don't forget to consider the psychological factors we talked about in Chapter Two. If your history is eradication and you want to change to mutual benefit, you may need to use a longer timeline than moving from mutual benefit to isolation.

Do you need to do a risk analysis so you know the risk of switching from elimination to containment? Is your VP of Sales going to get pissed and walk out the door because they've dedicated years of their life to destroying the competition, and now you're telling them to back off and get coffee with them instead? Understand all the risks of changing so you can have a plan to address each one. Essentially, follow project management 101.

As you make your project plan to start spreading the new tactics to the team, consider when and how you want to release information and to whom. You may need to lay some groundwork before you tell certain groups in order to change perspectives and reduce risk. People's identities are strong. Just because you've made a decision in a boardroom doesn't mean that your employees can change from enemies to friends (or vice versa) overnight.

Creating your plan uses all of the information we've covered in the book. Make sure that with every step of the way, you consider all four psychological factors, genetics, and past tactics. Once you have a plan, you can begin to consider how you want to respond to competitors' tactics against you.

CHAPTER TEN

RESPONDING TO COMPETITION

PREPARING FOR COMPETITION

Think back to your answers in Chapters Three and Nine. As you have determined the reality of your market situation and what makes the most sense for your company, now it's time to reverse it.

Start by asking yourself: what has my competition's response been, historically? If you have several competitors, they have had a range of responses, so be sure to review each individually. As best you can, you're trying to decide what you think they appear to be doing. Here are some questions to get you started:

- Are they trying to drive you out of business?
- Have they made overtures that they want to buy or acquire you in some way?

- Have we, without any tacit conversation, found ourselves in a mutual benefit situation?
- Do they consider it a zero-sum or win-win market?
- Do they bring market specialization or a segment you don't cover? (Or vice versa?)
- Are they interdependent or dependent (for the end product, service, or supply chain) on you?

It's just as important to consider all of these factors for your competition as it was to consider for you. Most people assume their competition wants to eliminate them from the market, and frankly, that may not be the best thing for them.

Then, ask yourself: what should their strategy be? Put yourself in their shoes. Once you think you know what your competition would do, then you can decide how you would counter that action. It takes a combination of (1) historic actions and (2) what the action should be before you can decide what you should do to prevent their actions from being successful.

However, remember that you need to take the actions of all of the players in the competition's company into consideration. If their competitive position isn't clear, their sales team may be incentivized to act in a way that doesn't make sense from a corporate perspective.

Once you know what your competition is trying to do, you can employ a counter-response.

ERADICATE

If you decide the competition is trying to eradicate you, you have two choices in response: defend or counterattack.

DEFEND

If you're looking to defend yourself against an eradication strategy, you'll want to stay towards the positive end of the spectrum of components, as your biggest defense is maintaining legitimacy within your market since that's what your competition is trying to destroy.

You can do this by reinforcing your identity and brand loyalty. Then, you can attempt to figure out your competitor's allies. It's often their customers, but it can also be suppliers or other competitors. Make sure to take a global look at the market: who are all the horizontal (advertising groups, legal teams, media, politicians) and vertical (direct customers, supply chains, distributors) stakeholders? Create a list of their potential allies and then consider how you can segment and appeal to those groups. Even if it's other competitors, the enemy of your enemy could be your friend.

Ensure your list covers every possible angle. There are probably horizontally-connected entities that aren't obvious from a first glance. If they dominate the advertising community, you might not be able to get your message heard. If they have political connections, they could unfavorably affect your business through zoning or taxes.

Don't forget the last possible group: the competitor itself. They could be behaving in a manner that doesn't make sense. An option is to sit down with their executive team and attempt to convert them from eradication to another response that's less aggressive—maybe offer an incentive.

A warning on defend: there is a possible pitfall to positive spectrum defending. You could be seen as weak and ineffective. However, it's less likely to backfire on you than a counterattack.

COUNTERATTACK

When you choose to counterattack, you'll need to move towards the negative end of the spectrum. Look out for opportunities to discredit the competition. The easiest way to do that? If they're already engaging in negative activities, call them out on it.

You can look at where they are vulnerable to public attack as well. Do they have outside investors that you don't have, so you can paint them as negative? Are they not contributing to the community? Do their products or services have a legitimate quality issue?

If none of the obvious actions work, you can try legal actions. You can sue them to create perceived legitimacy or harm them in some way. Or, you can disrupt their internal operations through actions such as stealing their talent or disrupting their supply chain.

Another tactic is to make them insignificant by changing the market itself. (If you want to use this tactic, I highly recommend reading *Blue Ocean Strategy* by Chan Kim and Renée

Mauborgne.) You don't need to have a major technology shift to change the market. Instead, redefine what value is in a market by creating a new value stream. If your competition can't get in on that stream, they become insignificant.

An example Kim and Mauborgne give in their book is the creation of iTunes. At the time there was a flood of illegal music through Napster, Kaza, LimeWire, etc. By 2003, more than two billion illegal files were being traded every month. Apple saw an opportunity. They made a deal with the five major music companies who were suffering from these illegal downloads and created iTunes, an easy to use platform that made it easy for consumers to purchase a single track and hold it in their hands with an iPod.

Apple took an underground illegal file sharing program market and redefined it. It appealed to their music company competitors and to consumers. By redefining the digital music market, they created blue ocean space—and they were prepared to dominate it with a consumer-friendly offering.

A warning on counterattacks: make sure you consider how you will be perceived by everyone in the vertical and horizontal chain. If you're the bigger company, it doesn't matter what they did to you, because you're the 800 pound gorilla. Your reaction, if seen as overly aggressive, could hurt your position in the market. This is known as the horizontal hostility effect (though it can be seen sometimes in the vertical chain to a lesser extent). If you "overreact," other competitors are more likely to bond together against you than to bond with you. After all, there's a natural tendency for so-called "little guys" to bond together.

AVOIDING MERGERS

Today it's very common for small and medium sized companies to be in a larger competitor's crosshairs for acquisition. If you think you may be in those crosshairs, you need to have an internal discussion at the leadership level (and probably throughout the company, depending on your size). How do you monitor the environment? How do you know you're in the crosshairs, and how do you get out of them?

A lot of the time the company looking to acquire you aren't even direct competitors—they're big holding companies or companies looking to expand as a way to cut back-office costs or reduce production costs.

If a company is trying to acquire you, they're going to come at you subtly. It wouldn't be in their best interest to discredit or weaken your company too much, as they'll want to make money off of you. Most likely, they'll result in threats or closed-door attacks.

If you don't want to be acquired, you can try to villainize them ahead of any aggressive moves they make, in order to dissuade them from coming into the market. You want to drive the point home to them that you're ahead of their organized strategy, and it would be too costly for them to even attempt to enter.

If you have a board of directors, you can also poison them against the potential purchaser: "These people are awful, they're not going to bring value to the community, and they'll ruin the business." You can go to the supply chain and tell them if the purchaser comes to town, they won't use them.

You can even go to your bank and explain, "You make a lot of money loaning money to my business. These guys don't need you and won't use you." Poison as many stakeholders and horizontal and vertical partners as possible against them as soon as they start considering entering your market.

However, if you know that they're going to come in and there's not much you can do to stop it, invite several other big companies to sniff around at the same time. This can either change all of their motivations to acquire you, or it can drive up your value. If you're going to get acquired, you might as well get the most money you can get.

ISOLATE

If you decide the competition is trying to isolate you, you have two choices in response: contain and counter.

CONTAIN

If your response is to try and contain the competition, you need to consider who they are. If they've achieved mastery in certain areas, you need to be realistic. You probably won't be able to match mastery.

Say your competitor is the Shouldice Hernia Hospital. You'll never be able to match their expertise and reputation, so you may not want to try to offer hernias. Instead, you should contain them to that specific mastery, and grab the rest of the market so they can only offer that single service or product.

The same idea applies to expertise. You can either invest in the R&D to outdo them in their area (but be realistic about how much it will cost and how long it will take), or you can ensure they only do that one service.

If the competitor has market dominance in one or more niche areas, in order to contain them, you would allow them to own some of those niches while you focus on growing in all the other areas instead. In essence saying, "You get this sector, and I'll take these."

COUNTER

If you want to counter mastery, options include affiliating with a bigger brand (in our hernia example, this could be Johns Hopkins or Mayo Clinic). This can help you "gain" the same level of mastery quickly.

Or, you can venture into the negative spectrum: discredit how they do things or expose weaknesses that consumers may not know about. However, the truth is that if they've achieved a high level of expertise or mastery, your chances of effectively countering that are pretty slim—or they'll require a tremendous amount of resources and effort.

When it comes to market dominance, to counter you could provide an alternative for every niche they are in to undercut their dominance. You may not need to develop these alternatives much, but by having them, you reduce their dominance while keeping them from expanding into your niches.

Also, think about visibility in the market. If you see a McDonald's on your street, chances are there's also a Burger King within a few blocks. For years, if Walgreens opened a store, a CVS would be built within visible eyesight. If your competitor puts up a sign, you put up a bigger one. If they open a store on this corner, you open one on the opposite corner.

The pitfall of this counter method is that it can lead to an arms race: who has the most capital to survive? So if you want to choose this counter method, make sure you have a clear strategy and are aware of your capital line because you're going to need a lot of it.

MUTUAL BENEFIT

If you decide the competition is trying to create mutual benefit with you, you have two choices in response: accept or deny.

ACCEPT OR DENY

Accept and deny are pretty straightforward. If someone is approaching you, consider what the benefits are to you and to them. Is it a win-win scenario? Or is it a better deal for them than for you?

If it's the former, acceptance could be a good route to take. If the latter, you may want to deny. If there's an imbalance in the relationship, one side could feel vulnerable—and that means it's unlikely to ever be a long-term successful relationship. For instance, if I own the entire supply chain and your existence is based on my willingness to sell you those supplies, you may want to enter into a mutually beneficial relationship, but you'll never be comfortable because you know I have absolute control.

When you want to deny an approach, however, make sure you ask yourself a few questions first. Do they control elements of the customer experience that you need or elements of the supply chain? If they do, you can tell them to take a hike, but you should think through their response first. They may respond by trying to eradicate you through acquisition or isolating you to the point where you can't grow anymore.

The question comes down to: what are the costs of saying no, and what are the benefits of saying yes?

Also, be sure to consider your historic position. If you want to say yes, but your employees have been trying to eradicate each other, you may have to talk to them about how to handle the situation. It may take more time to set up the situation. Or you may need a scapegoat—you see this often in mergers and both CEOs are fired, and a single new CEO is put in their stead.

HAVE A STRATEGY FOR EVERY SITUATION

It's essential to have a responsive thought process within the same framework that created your strategy. Think through every competitor's current and potential strategies and what new competitors might try, and have a strategy ready to be prepared.

As part of your yearly strategic planning process, plan your competitive position and strategies for the upcoming year, as well as three to five years out. What is your biggest risk—and what is your response to that risk?

This is an oversimplified way of looking at competitive positions, of course. You need to consider the details of each individual relationship. However, this should provide you with a basic framework to build your customized competitive plan on. And remember, the enemy of good is perfect. If perfection is your goal, you'll never release anything—we wouldn't have cell phones or laptops, or TVs. Make your plan and know that you may have to pivot as the landscape changes throughout the year.

CONCLUSION

At this point, you should have learned that the idea of competitive position is an essential component of your business. It's present, whether you recognize it or not. It's like the old David Foster Wallace joke,

> There are these two young fish swimming along, and they happen to meet an older fish swimming the other way, who nods at them and says, "Morning, boys. How's the water?" And the two young fish swim on for a bit, and then eventually, one of them looks over at the other and goes, "What the hell is water?"

WHAT WE'VE LEARNED

In Part One, you learned that competition is always present. It's an absolute, like air or water. It's part of your unavoidable environment. In fact, it's coded into your genetics. You, and every person on your team, is either a warrior or a worrier. And regardless of their genetic position, everyone is going to be influenced by four psychological factors: identity, relational, incentives, and ranking. Once you get through the genetic and psychological factors, you have to contend with the spectrum of components. Are your competitive behaviors on the positive side (through expertise, innovation, or price lowering) or the negative side (through discredit, threat, or disruption)?

In Part Two, you learned the three main strategies of competition. With eradication, you can either eliminate or acquire your competition. With isolation, you can either contain or counter your competitors. And through mutual benefit, you can either engage in market dominance or efficiency.

Lastly, in Part Three, you learned the framework you need to create your own competitive position and how to respond to competitive strategies from your competitors.

WHAT'S NEXT?

Now that you've finished *The Rules of the Race*, I want you to rethink your strategic planning sessions. Ask yourself, "Are we already considering these strategies during our yearly planning sessions?" If the answer is yes, great—thanks for reading! If not, it's time to decide how to incorporate this framework into your business strategy cycle.

Get together with your key team members and work through the questions I've asked you in this book. Define your position in the market and take a hard look at your competition. Get clear on your historic position and their historic position. Have clear, hard conversations that you've never had before. Don't just talk to the board or C-suite, however.

Involve people from all levels and departments of the organization. Remember, not every department will consider the competition in the same light. Plus, this affects the entire team. So you should decide how you include them in the process.

Consider the community when you make your decisions as well. If you decide to eliminate the competition and it's a small area, your employees' wives, brothers, and cousins may work for that competitor. While it may be the right business decision, you may want to initially limit the number of people you tell and think through the best way to inform the team when it's time to announce. Maybe you don't specifically announce your strategy but create incentives or rankings that will influence them to be more aggressive.

NEED HELP?

If you want more information about creating a competitive position or you want to listen to real-life examples from business leaders like you, visit my website at drbradarcher.com. There you can hear stories from others in our community— or you can share your competitive story with the community. You can also contact me directly by emailing me at info@ drbradarcher.com.

www.ingramcontent.com/pod-product-compliance
Lightning Source LLC
Chambersburg PA
CBHW030529210326
41597CB00013B/1076